T0199034

EXCITING BIBLE STORIES

FOR KIDS

REV. DR. SUE PERRY

WestBow Press books may be ordered through booksellers or by contacting:

WestBow Press
A Division of Thomas Nelson & Zondervan
1663 Liberty Drive
Bloomington, IN 47403
www.westbowpress.com
1 (866) 928-1240

Because of the dynamic nature of the Internet, any web addresses or links contained in
this book may have changed since publication and may no longer be valid. The views
expressed in this work are solely those of the author and do not necessarily reflect the
views of the publisher, and the publisher hereby disclaims any responsibility for them.

Any people depicted in stock imagery provided by Getty Images are models,
and such images are being used for illustrative purposes only.
Certain stock imagery © Getty Images.

ISBN: 978-1-9736-9456-4 (sc)
ISBN: 978-1-9736-9457-1 (e)

Library of Congress Control Number: 2020911528

Print information available on the last page.

WestBow Press rev. date: 6/24/2020

WESTBOW
P R E S S®
A DIVISION OF THOMAS NELSON
& ZONDERVAN

This book is dedicated to Jesus the Christ, Our Messiah and Redeemer by the power and Grace of our Heavenly Father and the guidance of His Holy Spirit.

A special thank you to my Godchild Jane Perry for her patience in computer help, to my friend and faithful prayer warrior Brenda Hudson And to my beloved husband Bill.

Table of Contents

Noah and The Ark

Many years ago, lived a man named Noah.

Noah had three sons, Shem, Ham and Japheth.

Noah was a good man. He obeyed God. However, the people who lived in his land were not good. They did not obey God.

Eventually, the people were so bad that God was very sad and he decided to send a flood to cover the land.

Noah knew God was very unhappy with all the wickedness and understood that God wanted him to build an ark.

WOW! Can you imagine if God wanted you to build and ark?

You would be very surprised and maybe afraid. However, Noah knew God would tell him exactly how to build the ark; Noah listened to God and obeyed Him.

He built an ark—a very, very, very big boat.

It had room for Noah, his family and many animals.

After the ark was built, Noah brought animals into the ark, lots of animals. In fact, two of every kind, male and female, giraffes, and tigers, and lambs, and birds, even monkeys and many more!

So, Noah brought into the ark males and females, giraffes and tigers and lambs, birds, monkeys and many, many more.

Then Noah brought in more animals --7 pairs of other kinds of animals, male and female.

Noah did everything he knew God wanted him to do.

Then it was time for Noah to take his family into the ark, and so he did just that. So, Noah obeyed. He took his family into the ark and God shut the door. Noah was 600 years old.

After Noah and his family went into the ark, it began to rain and rain and rain. It rained for 40 days and nights!

The whole earth was flooded and the waters covered the earth. Even the mountains were covered with water.

However, God lifted the ark high above the earth and it floated on the surface of the water.

Noah, his family and the animals were safe and dry.

Then God sent a wind over the earth and the water slowly went down and the ark rested on a mountain.

After 40 days, Noah opened a window and sent out a raven which flew back and forth.

Then he sent out a dove, but the dove could not find a place to perch so it went back to Noah.

After 7 more days, he sent the dove out again, it returned and this time it had a branch in its mouth! So Noah knew that the flood was gone.

After 7 more days, he sent the dove out again, but it did not come back. It had found a place to live.

Noah looked out of the ark and saw the dry land and knew it was time to come out of the ark with his family and the animals.

Noah obeyed God and everyone and every animal came out of the ark.

Then Noah built an altar to thank the Lord.

God was pleased with Noah and placed a rainbow in the sky.

Noah saw the rainbow and was reminded of God's great love and deliverance.

Today, when it rains, we can see God's beautiful rainbow and remember how much He loves us.

David and Goliath

There was a boy named David. He was the youngest of eight boys and he tended sheep for his father. He was a shepherd.

In the morning, he led the sheep out to the fields to be fed. They ate grass.

It was also David's job to protect the sheep. Sometimes, he had to fight off wild animals like lions and bears.

At night he guided the sheep into a pen for safety.

At that time, there was war between David's people the Israelites and the Philistines and David's brothers went off to fight with the army of the Israelites.

However, because David was the youngest, he stayed home to care for his father's sheep.

There were no restaurants in those days, so the families of the soldiers had to provide food for them.

One day David's father told him to take food to his brothers, see how they were doing, and come back and tell him. So David got up early left his sheep with another shepherd, took the food and went to see his brothers.

The war had been going on a very long time and the soldiers were getting discouraged.

The Israelites stood on one mountain and the Philistine stood across from them on another mountain. There was a valley between the two mountains.

One of the Philistine soldiers was so tall he was a giant! His name was Goliath. He was very scary and the Israelites were afraid.

He was also very rude. He would shout mean things at the Israelites.

One day, he was shouting challenges for someone to fight with him. If the challenger won, Goliath's army would be servants of Israel but, if Goliath won, the Israelites would be servants.

No one wanted to fight this giant. They were all very, very frightened.

The soldiers knew that the king would give them many riches and even let them marry his daughter; which was pretty cool in those days, if they would go fight the giant.

However, no one was brave enough to fight.

When David arrived at the camp, with food for his brothers, he heard about the giant and even heard the giant yelling at the Israelites.

David did not understand why the Israelites were afraid. He reminded the soldiers that they were the army of God and no one can defeat God so they should not be afraid.

When the king heard what David had said, he asked him to come see him and David did.

He comforted the king and volunteered to fight the giant.

But the king knew David was just a boy and Goliath was a giant.

But David told the king how he protected the sheep and even fought and killed lions and bears.

He told the king and praised God for delivering him from the lions and bears and knew that God would deliver him from the giant.

So the king agreed and he put a heavy helmet on David's head and heavy armor on his body and fastened a sword to the armor.

David could not walk with all that gear on him. So he took it all off.

Then he took his shepherd's staff in his hand and he chose 5 smooth stones from the brook, and put them in his shepherd's bag. He also had a sling in his hand.

Then he went out to meet the giant.

When Goliath saw David, he laughed and was rude because David was only a boy. He told David to come to him so he could kill him.

But David let him know that he was there because God was with him.

Then the giant walked toward David. David was not afraid. He knew God was on his side. So, he ran toward the giant and as he did he took one of his stones and put it into his sling. He swung it around and sent the stone right into the giant's forehead and the giant fell down dead!

When the giant's army, the Philistines, saw that the giant was dead they ran away.

David trusted God and God defeated the giant.

Daniel and The Lion's Den

Many years ago, the people of Israel were captured by a mighty nation. Daniel was one of the young men who were captured.

Because he loved the Lord God and obeyed Him, he became strong and very wise.

Therefore, although he was a servant of the king, because the Spirit of the Lord was in him, the king planned to appoint David over the entire kingdom.

Sadly, some people were very jealous of Daniel and wanted to get rid of him. They tried to find reasons to complain about him to the king. They could not find anything to complain about.

Therefore, they tricked the king into passing a law that said anyone who prayed to anyone except the king for 30 days would be thrown into a den of lions!

The king signed the law.

Although Daniel knew that the king had signed that law, he continued to go to his house and get down on his knees three times a day to praise the Lord and pray, just as he had done before the new law.

Now Daniel's house had windows that were open. People could see him when he prayed and the people who were trying to trap him into breaking the law could see that he was continuing to pray to God and not the king.

One day those men came and saw Daniel praying to the Lord God. Then they went to the king and reminded the King that he had signed a law that said anyone who prays to anyone, within thirty days, except to him would be thrown into a den of lions.

The king knew that it was true and that the law could not be changed!

So, those evil men made sure the king knew Daniel was still praying three times a day to his God.

When the king heard this he was very sad. He liked Daniel. He did not want to put him in the lion's den.

He was so unhappy and worried that he spent all day trying to figure out a way to save Daniel, but, he could not.

He knew the evil men were jealous of Daniel. They had tricked him into signing a law that could not be changed.

At the end of the day the men who did not like Daniel went to the king and said, "It is the law. You must put Daniel in the lion's den."

So, even though the king did not want to do so, he had Daniel thrown in the lion's den!

The king spoke with Daniel and hoped that his God who he faithfully served would save him.

Then a stone was brought and put at the mouth of the den and the king sealed it with his signet so that no one could free Daniel.

Then the king, very upset and sad, went to his bedroom. He did not eat all night and he was so worried about Daniel he could not sleep.

As soon as the sun began to rise, the king got up and hurried to the lions' den to see if God had saved Daniel from the lions.

He asked if God had saved him. Daniel replied that his God had sent his angel and shut the mouths of the lions so they would not hurt him because he had done nothing wrong.

Then the king was very, very happy and commanded his people to take Daniel out of the lions' den.

So Daniel was taken out of the lion's den and the lions had not hurt him at all because he had trusted God.

The king also gave a command that those who had plotted against Daniel be thrown into the lions' den and they were.

Then the king wrote to all the people about a new law. It said that all the people should honor God forever because He saved Daniel and because He is faithful and all powerful forever.

Jonah and The Big Fish

Jonah, a prophet of God knew that God wanted him to go to Ninevah because the people were being very bad. He knew that God wanted them to STOP being bad or their city would be destroyed.

Jonah did not want to go to Nineveh and he decided to run away. Everyone knows you can't run away from God. However, Jonah tried.

He went to a city called Joppa and boarded a ship going in the opposite direction of Nineveh.

Then the Lord made a very strong wind to blow and a big, very big storm began to toss the boat so much that it almost broke into pieces.

The sailors were very frightened and they started throwing their supplies into the sea so that the ship would be lighter and perhaps not sink.

The sailors met and tried to figure out whose fault it was that God had sent this tremendous, fierce storm.

They decided the storm was raging because of Jonah. Jonah was asleep!

The captain woke him up and asked him why he was sleeping. He wanted him to pray to his God so that they would not die.

They wanted to know where Jonah was from and why this was happening.

So he had to admit that he was a Hebrew, that worshipped the creator of all and he was running from Him.

Then the men were even more afraid. Jonah was trying to run away from God!

So, they asked Jonah what to do to stop the storm because it was getting stronger and stronger.

The wind was blowing and the waves were smashing against the boat.

Jonah knew God made the storm because he had disobeyed Him, so he told them to throw him into the sea.

At first, they did not want to do that. They rowed the boat harder and harder trying to get to land.

Still the storm became stronger and stronger so they prayed to God to save their lives and not to punish them for throwing Jonah into the sea.

Then they picked Jonah up and threw him into the sea and the wind stopped and the water became calm.

The men knew God helped them so they thanked him.

In the meanwhile, God sent a large fish to swallow Jonah and he was in the belly of the fish three days and three nights!

Ewww can you imagine being inside a fish? Probably not.

While Jonah was in the big fish, he prayed to the Lord God to save him. So God spoke to the big fish and it vomited Jonah out onto dry land.

Again, God told Jonah to go to Ninevah. This time Jonah obeyed. He went to Ninevah and warned the people to listen to God and be good.

They did and God forgave them and blessed them.

God is always faithful.

Joshua and Rehab

Many, many years ago there was a man named Joshua. Joshua loved God very much. When God told Joshua to go to a strange land and make it his home, Joshua obeyed.

That sounds very easy, doesn't it? And at first glance it might have sounded easy to Joshua. You see this land, the Promised Land that God had provided for His children the Israelites, had wonderful things in it; such as grape vines with grapes so big it took two men to carry a bunch!

Have you ever seen grapes that big? Nope.

God provided this land and it had marvelous blessings in it for His people. All they had to do was go there.

So what is the big deal? Just about anybody can move, especially if you know God is giving you a new wonderful home. Isn't that right?

Well, there was this one problem. The land had giants and the people of Israel were afraid. They forgot how powerful God is. They forgot to trust Him.

They forgot that God is stronger and more powerful than anything or anybody—even giants.

However, Joshua did not forget and he trusted God to protect him. He knew God can and will do surprising, wonderful things when we believe and trust Him.

Joshua obeyed God. He took his friend Caleb and went to check out the city called Jericho.

They had to be very careful because they were spying on the people and the land. A spy is a person that secretly looks for information.

Joshua didn't want anyone to see them and capture them. They were very, very careful and very, very quiet.

When the spies arrived in Jericho, they came to the house of a woman named Rahab. They went into her house and asked her a lot of questions about the city.

Now Rahab lived in a house with a window that looked out of the city into the country. And it saved Rahab's and the spies lives.

But I will tell you about that in a minute.

Another very good thing about Rahab's house was that it had a flat roof. On that flat roof, Rahab stored flax.

Flax is a plant that is dried and then made (woven) into linen cloth—pieces of material that skirts and shirts and other things are made of.

It was a very good thing for those spies that Rahab had flax on that very flat roof. You see the king found out that Joshua and Caleb were in his city and he sent a message to Rahab to send those men out of her house.

Well, what do you think Rahab did? Instead of letting the king capture the spies, she hid them on her roof under the flax!

The king's men could not find the spies and went away.

Then a wonderful thing happened. Rahab told the spies that she knew God had given the land to them.

She knew that God is wonderful and powerful and takes care of His people.

She knew that God is in heaven above and on earth below. He is everywhere.

So Rahab asked the men to save her and her family when they came to take over the city. And they did!

They told Rahab to hang a scarlet (dark red) cord in the window and to bring all of her family into her house.

Rahab trusted the spies and she trusted God, so she did exactly what she was told to do.

First, she let the spies down out the window. Then she tied a cord so it hung on the outside of the window and she brought her family into her house.

She believed and was saved as you will soon see.

Joshua and The Battle of Jericho

After Joshua and Caleb returned from spying on the city of Jericho, God told Joshua to march around the city with all his warriors once a day for six days.

Seven priests would carry seven trumpets and the Holy Ark of the Covenant would be carried with them. But they were not to blow the trumpets on those six days.

On the seventh day they were to march around the city seven times with the priests blowing the trumpets. When the people would hear the trumpets they were to shout.

So Joshua obeyed God. He had the people and the priests with their horns and the Holy Ark Of the Covenant march around the city once a day for six days.

They did not blow trumpets, they just marched.

Then on the seventh day, the people and the priests, with the Ark behind them, marched around the city six times. The priests blew the trumpets, but the people were still quiet.

On the seventh day, Joshua told them to march around the city and "SHOUT! For the Lord has given them the city.

So the people SHOUTED and the trumpets were BLOWN and an amazing thing happened, the walls of the city fell down flat! and Joshua and his people captured the city of Jericho.

They brought Rahab and all her family out of the city and they all went to live with the Israelites for Rahab had obeyed God and hidden the spies.

We can always trust God. He keeps His promises and acts in wonderful ways to bless us because He loves us.

When we keep our eyes on Jesus (we listen to Him and study the Bible and pray) we can serve God in exciting ways.

The King

There once was a very kind, loving king who lived in a beautiful kingdom, with His mighty and powerful Father.

In the land where the King and His Father lived, everyone was always happy and no one ever cried.

No one was hungry or thirsty because the King took care of all His people.

They were never lonely because He was always with them.

They were never afraid because He always protected them. AND it was never dark!

This king had other people that did not live with Him. He loved these people so much that one day he left His throne and went to live with them.

He walked with them, visiting women, men and even little children. He told about his beautiful land and most of all about His loving Father.

Even though He was a king, He had dinner with them and held the children on His lap. He might have even told them bedtime stories and maybe tucked them in for the night.

However, this king wasn't content (happy) to just visit these people or to be on vacation with them. He wanted them to live with Him in his kingdom. But He knew they couldn't do that because to live in his kingdom you had to be very, very good. You had to be perfect.

No one could be mean or selfish.

No one could lie or steal.

Certainly no one could be rude or get into arguments. And He knew they had all done these things. Some had even killed other people!

He loved them anyway.

Whenever He visited with the people He told them how much He loved them and how He wanted them to love Him and be with Him.

He told them how to love each other and be kind to each other. He told them over and over how much His Father loved them, better than prince charming loved Cinderella, better than Romeo loved Juliet, better than anyone any time ever loved anyone, His father loved them more.

Even though the King fed the hungry people, made the sick people well and the sad people happy, sadly, many people did not understand how much He loved them.

So, the King told His friends, like you and me, to tell everyone how much He cared for them. Then He invited them all to be his people in his kingdom!

Wow! Can you imagine living with a king?

Remember the King knew these people had a tendency to get into trouble. He also knew that no one ever, ever was naughty in his kingdom. He told them how very important it was to be good.

But many people did not believe Him. You see, every time someone did something they were not supposed to do, like lie, or steal, or fight there was a punishment and there was no way they could make up for all the things they had done wrong. So they could not go to his home and kingdom.

The worst part was that the punishment for their sins was death! They were doomed.

However, this King loved these people and He wanted them with Him for always and forever. So He decided that He would take the punishment for all the people; not just one or two or three or four but all of the people!

Would you want to be punished for what your friends did or your brother or sister or the people who don't like you? No, you would not.

Nevertheless, that is exactly what this King did. He agreed to be punished for their sins. He died **<u>for them.</u>**

This King had never ever done anything wrong. But He loved the people so much, (even the ones who did not love Him) He loved them so much that **He died so they would not have to die. AND** they could go to live with Him.

How could that be? He was dead. This king, who said He loved them and wanted them to go and live in his kingdom and have their very own mansions, was dead.

Everyone knows you can't do anything if you are dead!

Dead is dead.

Well, this was no ordinary King. This was the Son of God. He was more powerful than death. And even after they buried Him, his love was so strong, He came back to life!

He visited his friends and told them how much He loved them.

He ate with them. He proved He was alive!

He told them to tell everyone and let them know they were invited to be with Him forever in his kingdom.

This mighty King is JESUS. His Father is God.

He wants you to know He loves YOU so much that He died for you and even death wasn't strong enough to keep Him away from you!

He wants you to believe in Him and some day come and live with Him in heaven.

He took your punishment and made it possible for you to come and live with Him. The gates of heaven are open and your mansion is waiting for you.

All you have to do is to believe in Jesus, that He is the Son of God, to give Him your life and trust Him. Then you can be with Him forever.

Amen.

Rev. Perry and her husband Bill (retired Navy) are the parents of 7 children, 25 grandchildren, and 6 great grandchildren and 2 more on the way.

They live in North Carolina, USA and love the Lord with all their hearts and souls.

Printed in the United States
By Bookmasters